EGG-ONOMICS

BY ERIC SAMUEL M

EGG-ONOMICS EXPLAINED

"Eggonomics", a holistic new model for understanding the functions in our natural and synthetic social structures and activities, will show us how current measures of historical Economics will interact, shift, effect and "shock" each-other by utilizing the already known 'Schedules' of Economics. This system of merging a Natural System, (an egg), with a Synthetic System, (engine or machine of finance), will further our growth patterns, Returns of Investments and the ongoing study of Economics, science of trade-offs and choices, itself.

This 'egg model' visually lays-out methodological and analytical cause-and-effect theories that can be proved either by definitive mathematical properties or by continued research and study of global enterprise. By utilizing the same exogenous and endogenous measures of Micro- and Macro- fields of Demand, Supply, Price Levels and Expectations, Revenue (or Returns), Costs, Possibilities and Behaviors of Production Functions and the Values of these Inputs- Land, Labor, Capital, and Knowledge (or Technology), and such Outputs, such as Income, Wealth, Economic Growth, Consumption, Taxation, International Expenditures and Involvements, Employment Markets, interest rates and Wages, to better regard and know our Human systems.

It will also offer a 'better read' of Economic Theory, to assist all World's Leaders of Business and Government to continue the struggle to gain mutual respect, benefits, hope and honor for a prosperous and peaceful existence. Our mechanisms have our mucked-up our soils and clouded our skies, let's try growing something new, 'from the ground up'. We are 'of Nature' after all!

SUPPLY

To understand how the Supply Schedule functions among these "aggregate" measures of GDP, Price Levels (Inflation/Deflation), and Employment Demand, is to know the functioning and quantities of all sellable Goods and Services. 'Supply' is a 'bending down', upward sloping curve, steadily decreasing as, 'The Law of Decreasing Marginal Returns' presents the reasons for a downward sloping Demand Curve, (and the only formal 'Law' of Economics, aside from Carnegie's "Law of Growth", 'one must grow, for standing-still is like falling behind'). It is also based on Perfectly Competitive, Competitive, Oligarch-ich, market structures as well as the few "Perfect Monopolies", which will increase competition that breeds higher Supply levels and further choices of supplement goods and services, and also, innovation and imitations bring in new forms and avenues Supply, thereby decreasing the original 'Supply Side' to lessen or bend-in 'Quantity'.

With mathematical properties, measuring these 'moving parts or functions', like Velocity and then Acceleration, one could quantify 'acceleration' of Marginal Product of Labor, from a 'velocity' of Production Possibilities with an outer-most-bound 'efficient' Labor Demand from an MP_L, finding 'Equilibrium' in the Labor Market. This is the 'chalazae' of the Economic Egg, the 'stabilizer' and looks like this:

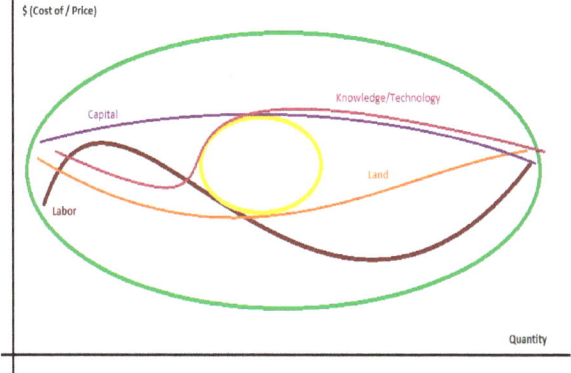

DEMAND

The very easily defined, yet hard-fought battle of 'Demand' or the "Demand Curve", utilizing the two-planer geometric scale, 'X' (the independent) and the 'Y' axis, (or dependent variable) has 'Quantity' and 'Price' (or '$'), as the only measurable "Qualities" of this behavioral Science. 'Time', 'Rates of Interest' even the differences between 'Cost' and 'Price' are not presently included in modern Economic Analytical Theory. As we say in baseball, 'The field is wide open!'

The Demand Curve is 'downward sloping' due to The Law of Decreasing Marginal Returns, or, after twenty scoops of ice-cream, at one sitting, the 'Value' of 'just one more scoop', has dropped dramatically! Put in theoretical terms, to sell more loafs of bread, (the plus one more batch or bag), the 'Price' to customer must drop, 'incentive-ising' the buyer to forego that 'next dollar'. 'Downward Sloping Demand Function' has recently been proven by increasing Revenues of companies that have dropped prices or, on the large 'Macro-Scale', "Decreasing Price Levels" and then the Consumer faces 'Expectations of Decreasing Price Levels"!

Our 'Egg model', places the Demand Curve or Function, *OUTSIDE* of The Egg, or 'Exogenously', for 'Demand' on a 'Global World Scale' is an outside force, one effected not only by containable 'Market Forces' or solely by 'Industry Standards', ie., The Labor Market for that Industry, or Costs and Price Fluctuations, but by something 'else' *Outside* 'The Market'. This is why J.M. Keynes was unsure of 'Deflation' being either a positive or negative force on 'Value', 'Full Employment' and 'Macro-Price Structures'. Simply put, 'Demand' surrounds and affects "everything".

Think of breakfast, two eggs, every day for a year, over easy, an omelet, scrambled, pouched, basted or fried, what would 'price expectations' be for eggs for breakfast and lunch? Add an obligatory 'eggs for dinner' intervention of 'law' and then, what would the 'Market Schedules' be for eggs? Can I interest you in a hard-boiled egg sandwich for dinner?

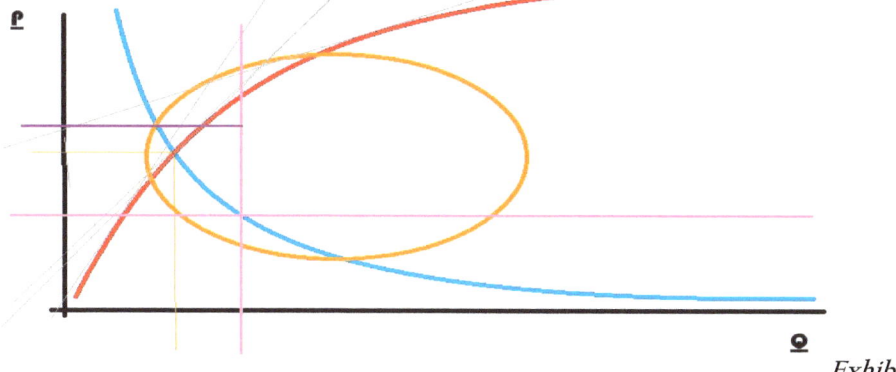

Exhibit "A"-

'Placement of the Economic Egg' –E.S. 10.10.14

-"Equilibrium" of 'Supply'/'Demand', and the new "thru" the Goods and Services Schedule of "The Egg's" 'Albumen'

(pls. note the decreasing Supply Tangents w/ new tendencies for greater Output w. only small Price decreases from The Egg)

VALUE

Value, the 'amount' a thing desired, at a rate of service- i.e. labor per hour, is "worth", in Quantitative terms has escaped Economists throughout history. Once thought to be based upon Land Use, or 'how much' a parcel of land can yield, then thought about 'how much' a 'worker can produce', this measure of worth, a "Price" of quantification has eluded the best and the brightest thinkers and theorists, until now!

Value equals, Utility MINUS the additions of Expectations ('environment'), plus Returns (Revenue) divided by Supply. In mathematical terms, $V = U - (E+R) / S$.

This should help to clarify 'inflated/deflated', 'under or over-valued' Qualities and Measures in Economics, Finance and Government. It is by no means the most correct or 'last word' of Price Theory nor the 'Absolute Truth' in the ongoing work of 'Evaluation Theories', but it is the latest formula for 'Value' and hopes to add to the problems of 'Preference Theories' and 'Worth/Wealth' problems.

UTILITY

Utility seems best described as 'Need' plus 'Desire', multiplied by 'Affordability'. The 'flip-mode', (props to Busta Rhymes…pls don't sue over 'flip-mode'- Much 'sPEct Due!). In Financial Terms, the Dependant and Independent Variables 'flip', Price being the main concern when 'shopping for Value', THEN, the purchased amount of 'Supply' follows, 'flipping' these 'Schedules'. Do the math, it is bound to shock!

'LAY-OUT' COMPARISON, OR 'MAP'

What good would general 'directions' be, without a 'map'? Here is what has been discussed so far:

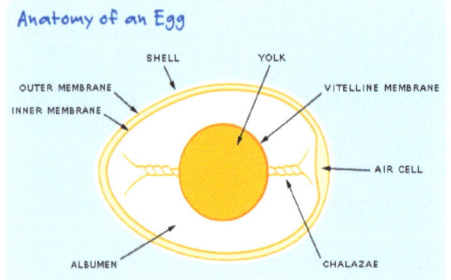

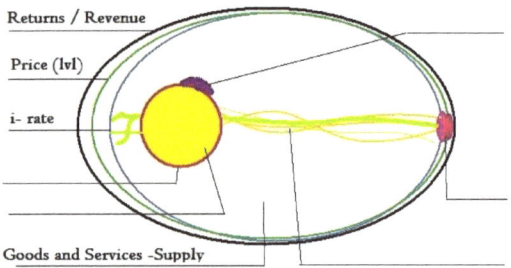

GROWTH

The 'growth' of this Economic Egg model will show and multiply what will work, what won't, what 'issues' are affectuated, effected, and what can and 'should' be done. As World's Leaders separate and combine actions, thoughts and deeds, along with cultural ideologies, 'yoke of custom' A. Marshall called it, we will continue to need 'Global Growth', a 'higher GDP Output', and basically need progress in every field.

To 'move' this global growth, with this new model, along, these new ideas contained in the following pages, will "shift-out" Supply, geometrically increasing 'Demand', cause 'higher Outputs' in every function, across every 'board' and 'farm house', 'little house' and Main Street to 'Wall Street' and beyond. It will 'increase in the entire quality of Wealth, Living, Employment, Price Stability, Cost and Price Structures, and the people of Earth will finally reach some hard discussed and hard measured conclusions, that we are indeed, already on a new path, a "Modern Economy" [ME], already filled with rich and vast demographicies, 'flourishing' with new ideas and contraptions for society, commerce, technology, labor movements and yes, even 'households'.

We <u>need</u> to look at things differently, a 'shift' or 'shock' in our perceptions or perspectives! As we can now all agree, 'Necessity' is the 'Mother of all invention'. It's not just an apple, or feisty little robot, or "kitch" attitude or awareness, it's an ongoing 'search', sometimes, 'trial and error', 'fight and flight' for 'the betterment of all Mankind'.

As our 75-85%+ of Global Market Investitures, Capital Inputs, and Financial Participation of the 'World's Markets', and the 'Financial Markets', Dow Jones, MIB, TASE, CAC, DAX, Hang-Seng, FTSE, NIKKEI, La Borsa, IBoveSpa, and the rest, have 'gone dry' from 'Mom-and-Pop' small investors, hopeful 'young entrepreneurs', 'recent grads' and 'whiz's' this steady decrease into global capital suicide, by way of 'self-fulfilling prophecy' will not only continue, but fall into an abyss of ill-liquidity and general revolt.

Have you ever worked in a kitchen with a very angry Chef or cook? It's not fun, nor 'efficient'! Things get broken, 'egos' and dangerous, hot objects get thrown, food burnt and wasted, and plates tossed, not in a fun, cultural way either! 'Growth' will only occur in positive, 'happy times' of defeat in war enemies, 'expansions' of Capital, and 'added' Land securities and fine, stable structuring, of which we have none and 'are out of'. History shows that when 'odds' of warfare, famine, disease and dys-functionality, 'the world' will whip-up a frenzy of hyper-death, mass-sacrifices, and following a 'General Agreement on Peaceful Tithes and Treaties'. Growth, prosperity, innovation, institutions and academic introspections abound! But now, as can be recalled, 'we have no bananas,' we are not in a state of 'slap me, and I'll smack you back". Our now, semi-peaceful, 'Global Community', 7,8,10 or 20, all intertwined and inter-connected, relying steadily upon each other, brings a new time of 'rebirth', 'reprise' and 're-structuring' of Human thoughts, theories, academia and ideologies. Isn't this what most have done throughout, Adam Smith, David Ricardo, Mills, Marshall, Jevons, Walrus, Marx, Vernon Smith, HG Wells, J.M. Keynes, Aldous Huxley, John Lennon, Solow, and so many others, have done, take these multi-faceted, intertwining, 'growth spurts', take out some of the pain, and continue on 'to that good night', without blood baths, bombings and beheadings? Stoned should We be, if we fail our Future's 'Growth Paths', for consideration and promises for 'common decency' and mutual-respectfulness for a new, but unsteady, 'Global Village' or 'World Enterprise' of 'yes, We can'. 'We' can provide 'Us' food, shelter, clothing, safe passage thru the world, honor-in-work and home and an overall, abundant and lasting, 'love of life'. Or, Maslow shall win, and we all suffer and die, fruitlessly.

'Growth', or the steady, sustainable Land, Labor, Capital, Knowledge Outputs abundantly occurring, will be, or, 'it will be', either soon, or'not-soon-enough', or, after we have all 'departed'. The question I have laid down to gauntlet is, how are 'We' going to affect or, 'be' the positive, sustainable, steady, and desired efficiencies in the Human Race of Capital, land, Labor and Knowledge? How will 'Our time on Earth' be remembered? I choose 'Value'! I choose 'mutual respect' or 'positive sum gains', or 'one boat for all of us'.

COSTS OF PRODUCTION

Production Costs stem from the 'Factors of Production'. Our only theory on this is that Labor is the only Factor that can change or be manipulated 'in the Short Term-Run'. This simply is not so in 'modern times'. Example submitted is the use of computers, either last Century or in this our beginning 'Millenniumhouse of Customs'. Can I not enrich the reader by a better use of 'paper-stock', higher in quality and quantity of pulp? Can you, a maker and supplier of Goods and Services rendered, not quickly and efficiently produce substantially improved Marginal Product by 'adding' simple Capital Investments such as 'cash infusions' or, computers, satellite views, "Magic Jacks" or faster, freer connections to the world wide web? Do you not incur 'additional' costs, marginally, like that of an 'additional worker', set also to become less attractive and useful by keeping with the Law of Diminishing Marginal Returns? Does anyone still believe we are like marmots' cousins, 'squirreling' away nuts, one at a time, in a 'technology-hole' once bore-d out and utilized for that 'run'? No, this is 'irrational', 'unsustainable' and 'corrupt' thinking!

The 'positive' or 'growth friendly' version of 'Short Run' costs are as follows: Ideological costs- one's first Labor cost, 'the one with the gold, makes the rules...' what then shall I do..., Structural Costs-otherwise known as 'Fixed Costs' of doing commerce ie., the lights, rent, transportation constraints and of course 'the run' of raw materials to make this 'production run'. Are mega-large 'firms' different? Does Coca-Cola or HP Printers and computers different in this 'economic restraint' of 'having to pay the piper'? No, I think that 'depreciation' and 'deflation' of quality and quantity served actually costs these mega-firms more, Short Term over 'the Long Run or Haul'.

This is merely an exercise in the quest to 'more efficiently gain, trap and grow' profits. This 're-direction' of thought is meant to 'spur' the Economy and large businesses who hire our neighbors and police, put teachers to salary and pay by way of insurances and re-assurances the fire and library departments.

Wasn't Adam Smith 'Inquiring' what makes a Nation wealthy? Isn't it 'the stock' of our respective Societies? What good would any of our 'Labor' be without time for a Coke, or workable matrix jet printer? Where would our 'social fabric' be without an afternoon Compari or Mint Julip or any 'Spirit' of Mankind's

Nature? If it be true that 'idle hands are the D_vil's playground,' that what be "overwrought hands on G_d's Green Earth?"

The Costs, of increased Marginal Productivity, are being seen world-wide, in the Under-Employment, low wages for too-many-unskilled hands, lowered pay-scales for the 'highly educated' and 'highly advanced', and add the ever-increasing Human Labor Supply and technical advancements of automation and 'self-serve' machinery, we see vast Unemployment, decreasing Wages, decreasing Price levels (to support this "new" deflationary environment) and continued 'stress' on the population, the 'system', businesses, governments and all 'institutions'. It's like an experiment badly planned and not questioned at all, what does 'a mouse' do if led down one path with a cheese on a string? 'Do he bite'? This 'common wisdom' without 'Questioning' or Oversight has brought us to many brinks of destruction and atrocities, dare we yet question 'the experiment'? Dog will hunt! But will he chew in time?

Time, the fervent 'enemy' of all humans, has costs and returns of all sorts. We have no time or scope to discuss the costs and prices of 'Time' here.

Labor Costs are quantified in 'Wages' either 'Real' or 'Wage Levels' or 'Nominally'. It seems unwise to 'pay' someone a lot or 'so much' to do so little. This is still the Economic measure of 'Diminishing Labor Returns' and seems to follow the discipline of the science, except that the 'Opportunity Costs' or 'The Worker' have never been formally calculated -in. "I write, therefore, I starve", and I can barely live with that! 'Value' was termed in the 'Human Capital' form of 'The Artisan', a painter who paints only 'masterpieces' of work so 'valuable' due to beauty, substance, demandable allure and scarcity, that its 'Price' only increase.

But, dare we 'predict' what happens to 'the Labor pool' or Labor Supply when population, education, skill levels of age, dexterity, intelligence, introspection, natural talents and even 'street-smarts' collude against 'The Job Seeker', with fewer skills to maneuver and less levers to pull? What happens when an unstoppable object meets an unmovable one? This mechanics question is 'irrational' Economists, as 'a fervent Outcome' is a must!

Costs of 'the unknown', of the 'under-educated' or under-trained, have compounded our recent Crisis. Costs, quantifiable, or only highly qualitative, hold 'the middle' together, being defined here as 'the chalaze' the 'structural support' of our 'Economic Egg'. Costs are what drive future Expectations of 'Prices', 'Supply Levels', 'Wages' or new, 'Non-Wage Earners' to a 'Sustainable' or 'Non-Sustainable' structures to support "the house". For every 'Marginal Cost' increase in just 'Labor Costs' alone, the 'Marginal Cost Curve' will 'tighten', and not only Shrink 'Profitable Supply' quantities based upon the Competitive Market profit maximization model of 'MR=MC' and stop production, but this 'tighter' Marginal Cost Curve also decreases efficiencies in Employment Demand, 'New Orders' of other Goods (and Services) and thereby starts to 'shrink the egg', "pulling" the entire Egg Structure as well as Supply and Demand Schedules 'back' towards zero or 'Y' bar. Therefore, the only Production deemed 'profitable' is a 'sustain' known Revenue patterns, thereby not 'growing' or 'pushing forth' and _breaking_ the only other known Economic Law, "Carnegie's Law of Growth", that to not improve, financially or socially, is by definition, to either stand still and stagnate, or lesson and rot, with Inflationary Pressures, Competitive and Predatory Pressures abounding, 'grow or die'.

Our current stasis is apt to wither and mulch, as seen by the recent Japanese 'lost decades', or, 'turn the cheek' to utilize friendly 'Non-competitive terms' to better cheaply Supply the Factors of Production, Land, Labor, Resources of Capital (financing), Knowledge (of Technology, 'know-how', and intelligent 'innovation'). This 'broadening' of Structural-ization, 'fabric of the Foundations' and increase of Macro-Supply and continued 'Price Dampen-ing' will bring-forth faster and better Opportunities for Growth.

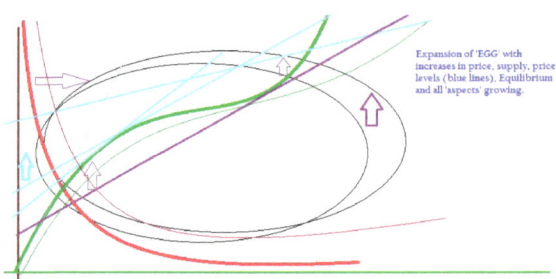

Expansion of 'EGG' with increases in price, supply, price levels (blue lines), Equilibrium and all 'aspects' growing.

'The Egg' expansion, showing 'Growth' in all 'Aspects' or all Schedules rising,

'Contraction' would be the opposite, with all Schedules 'shrinking'.

In times of 'Contraction' the opposite of 'Growth', 'The Egg' of Economics will expand out to the right of the Price and Quantity axes, Supply can 'remain' at static levels, while 'Demand' at each Price Level (in blue), will fall, due to short run turnarounds of Durable and Semi-Durable Goods. The now, newly mandated U.S. Fed Bank 2% overall, year-over-year' Inflation Target is based on these blue Supply tangent lines, showing the increases (or showing backwards- Prices decreasing), due to the impending Diminishing Marginal Returns. This is surely measured first in the Marginal Cost Curve, (MC), as 'more the labor added eventually reaches a undesirable Labor Demand Schedule at a point of dis-profiabiliity', or where MC=MR. These decreasing efficiencies, usually measured first, in the Production Possibilities Curve, which shows the Costs of Opportunity to 'invest (Capital and/or Labor) at a better Return rate', by allowing disproportions in the Comparative Advantage Schedule and 'too many cooks in the kitchen'. This is why we now see vast decreases in Prices and overall Demand in the Electronics Industry and many others, that the one 'Law' of Economics sets in, and just how many laptops, high-def. T.V.s, or plasma phones can one household or firm support? New markets *might* supply a new Demand of readied Supply, but, at what Price Level? Surely, the 'yoke of custom' as A. Marshal coined, will show that each 'Economy' will demand its own dish.

World's Leaders are currently hunting for growth in Supply and Demand, perhaps at higher Price Levels, perhaps at a Price stasis, but Inflation cannot be sustainable without a steady rise in 'Income', either by higher Returns to 'Investments' or 'Wage Levels' or both, this, a 'Quality' of mathematics, the un-affordability across all income levels and industries, is solved by 'The Egg' in an "Organic" fashion.

The Economic Egg doesn't hold to these 'obvious hidden anomalies' or ' black swans', akin to 'intuitive logic' the Marginal Product of Labor, and thereby, MC, and so, 'Profitability' of every business and Macro-Economic chart and prediction, is based on the Labor Market, as "in the Short Run scale, Capital is held as a constant (Factor of Production) rate, not to be inputted into the Output (Y) factorings, and so, only Labor (L, or N in most Economic textbooks) is counted. Therefore, 'Labor', the supply of and demand for is essential in the management, production rates, predictions and perpetuity of businesses and Output (Y), and also 'supplies' the "world's Labor force' with Income and Investment, that is 'time served for a 'Wage''.

The other two inputs, also not 'counted' in the Short-Run of Production, Cost Structuring and Output are, Land (here, 'N'), and Knowledge ('G'!?), as they are introduced to Economists as 'non-movable' or 'manageable' in the Short Run, which, by the way, Economics has yet to define as a rate of Time, ('T'). Land, N, is sometimes 'hard to come by' and yes, takes considerable Time to procure and ready for Production of Goods and Services, and often has considerable 'barriers to entry', so that should remain counted as 'fixed' in a 'Short or First or Second (Production) Run'.

Capital, 'K', might be counted as fixed or 'available' (or 'attainable') in the S.R., because of a full availability to add, 1. new materials to production; 2. Human Capital (probably counted as 'Labor', either in 'Management' or 'hourly labor' Services, and 3. Money, either 1,2,3 or 4 ('i.o.us'), schedules, sometimes easy to 'acquire' sometimes, not so easy.

Knowledge, 'G', is always with Humans, sometimes readily available, sometimes, no. This 'Input

Factor, seems to be a function of Time, Availability of Resources and Experience, Training (also Experience) and use and functionality of Technology, Human Labor of Capital, Capital (again, Technology and availability to others Factors of Production- Money, Land, Labor, Knowledge), and Culture, i.e., why Japan makes better "Japanese engines and Japanese watch movements, 'Made in Japan', than does Peru, Peruvian engines and Peruvian watch movements', "Hecho en Peru!". This is 'the heart' of "Comparative Advantage".

WAGES / INCOME

What would an Economy be without 'Earnings'? 'Income' for most, comes from 'Wages'. As of yet, we do not 'discount' or factor-in long-term 'cost-savings analysis', either endogenous or exogenous lowered Wage levels, powers of 'Collective Bargaining' either from Labor Unions or Firms with 'Purchasing Power' or from added extra costs, or benefits, from either side of the Labor Market. It is left, as any other production input or commodity to be priced with 'the Demand for' and/or 'Supply of', so determined. Labor is not as heavily regulated as is 'Capital Stock', Debt, Land-use or Rent nor is it measured in Quality as Capital, Knowledge or Land, and this all skews and confuses the problems and 'solutions' to our 'Labor Jobs Market'.

Included in a 'willing, readied and well-trained labor pool', is, at any Wage-Rate is 'Savings', as to be measured without the aid of 'Capital Investitures' of Stocks, Bonds, Equities and/or Large Assets, due to current conditions of Institutional 'Retirement Plans', either by "Companies" or "Government Guarantees". Also, as more workers 'Invest' more time and energy to their jobs, there is an increasing loss of time and (patience?) to participate in Pensions, retirement programs, research and 'time-off' to involve and investigate new or 'tried-and-true' "Avenues of Investment". In the terms of 'Opportunity Costs', there is only so much time, energy, Capital, and Knowledge of 'Moral Hazards' for 'the average worker' to investigate and involve one-self to making 'Savings' into 'Good Investments' with less the Risk and more the 'Secure Investment'.

Also, 'Incomes' at any level help to support the greater "Public Good", with Tax Collections, 'Public Works', 'Philanthropy' either at small or grander scales, social and/or religious involvements cause a 'money-multiplier' effect in liquidity, Money Supply, Confidence and a general well-being of each Economic Society.

Wealth, as measured by Capital or M_1, M_2, M_3, etc. (plus 'Values' of secondary and 'black markets'), and Land Values (seen negatively in the Current Global Financial Crisis), or other 'Durable' Assets, is mostly entirely built upon Wages, or "Investments" either of Capital-Stock (like an owner of a business) or Trades of 'Assets' of Equities or 'Self-Investments', like new 'small business owners' (which includes one's own specialized Labor plus their Capital invested), and/or 'Intellectual Property Investments' such as inventions, new Technologies, Ideas in Print, Film or Audio and other Formats, such as this book or 'The Beatles' or all of our recent 'Personal Computers' Industry, Windows, Apple Computers, the ideologies of 'Marxism' or the plethora of Financial Advice books on sale. A lot of Wages also comes for 'extra' sources of Employment, 'Holliday Bonuses', or 'Benefits' of Health Care, Child Care, connections to training, 'Industry Leaders' and 'Heads of State', are some of the un-quantified "earnings" of positions and 'Labor'.

Wages are a cost to 'the Labor purchaser', as the 'wage earner' "commands" or 'price takes' this Wage to forego Time for other Opportunities or other work. This 'Cost' of a 'Production Factor', still is counted as the only 'Short-Run' Cost in 'modern Economics' and is not discounted thru as other 'wage-earners' are hired, at lesser rates or as other Economic commodities are counted by 'Marginal Costs back-counted'. And, as Wages are being generally decreased year over year, for job-parity, on a global basis, 'higher world population', 'greater education, knowledge and techniques' are also putting 'downward pressures' on Wage Levels and hiring, decreasing both Labor Costs and 'Earning Potentials' of workers.

Income, whether "fixed", 'debt' or simple 'Wages', is the 'Yolk Sack' of our Egg Model. It holds-in the building materials of 'Consumption', the 'Yolk'. Income pays for production costs or 'the cost of living'.

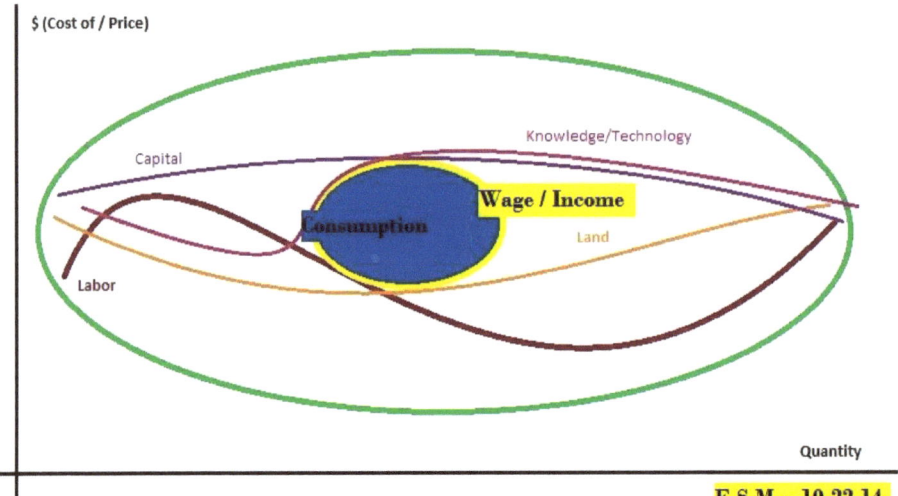

Consumption effects of 'Income', 'Wages Earned', 'Leveraged income' and 'Consumption' of Production or Living Costs.

CONSUMPTION

'Consumption' is extremely vital to 'The Economy', local, greater or global, as spending increases the Money Multiplier, The Expectations of "the Health" of an economy, further spending and Goods and Services traded. It balances 'Costs' of Labor, Goods and Services (sometimes measured in GDP), and even 'Savings' or funds which are not Consumed or Taxed.

Consumption here is 'The Yolk' of The Egg, and is paramount to: 1. Quantity (Sold), 2. Price Expectations (or Market Price Per…), and 3. "The Heat Index", or general Health of 'The Economy'. How much "we" spend, affects and guides the rest of what is bought, sold, held or traded.

Depending on how 'Qualities' move or shift in each Economy, will 'bend' or shift each 'Schedule' according to expected Laws of Nature. This (hopefully) "Outward" or Growth Trend will look like this, affecting each Schedule as per the arrows in an outward or positive direction, according to planer functions.

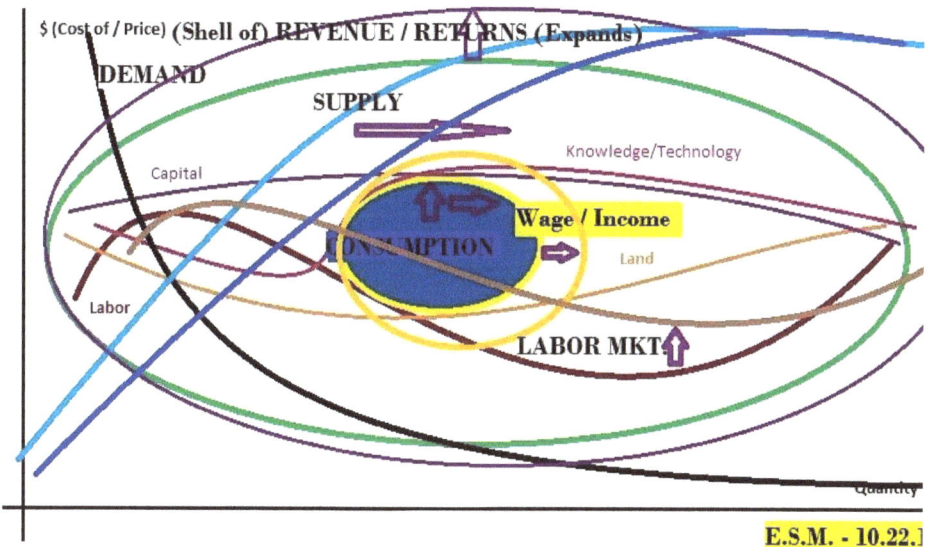

As 'Consumption' grows or expands, Wage / Income levels grow from furthered 'Expected Growth of Supply', or what happens to Goods and Services in a 'Inflationary-Productive Economy', like we're aiming for now. Supply or 'Overall Supply' or 'Supply Schedule' increases or expands due to increased spending, as seen in Post Great Depression Era, 'Mass Stimulus Packages' outlays, or 'Expansionary Practices' of Private Enterprise. This explains the 'Trickle Down' theory, that when more businesses spend and grow, so does the Overall Economy "spend and grow". The opposite can most be seen from recent 'Austerity' and 'cut back' policies.

As noted just above, The Labor Market will also expand as 'Wages/Income' grows, creating not only stable 'Wages' from both eager, well-trained Labor Pools, also from firms as Expectations of Supply grows. There is the extra-benefit of a positive 'self-fulfilling prophesy', as noted in business schools of the 'Henry Ford Effect', paying higher than Market Wage to induce higher Consumption, and 'fuel the local Economy'.

Growth in Consumption may also lead to higher Investitures in other regards such as 'Equity Purchases', 'Capital Goods', both Durable and Non-Durable, investments in smaller 'start-up' businesses, commercial and/or home Real-Estate, as 'surety' will be confidently boosted. There is also a benefit of lower 'Risk Ratios' once a 'known growth path' has been discerned. "Riskier" Assets are no longer as risky.

Demand Schedule from this Consumption Growth pattern, may or may not 'Shift' out or up, as "there are so many moving parts to an Economy", but, as labeled in this new 'Egg Model', even a 'line of sight' visual analysis can be useful to help determine a direction of a causational or effectual 'movement' or 'shift'. A "higher" Demand Curve will, of course, also 'boost' Expectations of Growth, Consumption (by definition), Supply and Price stabilities, as well as The Labor Market, Durable and Non-Durable Goods (and Services) Markets.

All and all, 'Consumption Growth' is alike a rise or growth in 'Demand', as almost always positive and 'spurring' of further Economic Growth and Positive Activity. A word on 'positive' growth, as per Consumption, Demand, Supply, Wages and Income, is "Incentive" or "Incentives", as the Science of Economics is based, on 'positive' and 'normative' study and analysis of personal, institutional, and social "Incentive" to 'Act'. Why would one bother to trade- sell or buy, rather than 'hold' and keep his coconuts or bananas to "himself", if the 'Valuations" were wrong or 'off'? The positive sum (gain) or 'Game', all involved winning, other "Games" of theory, code and position, are built in practice, to have the 'players' continue playing. Not one, 'Long-Term' is served by 'bad games'. 'bad rules', or 'faulty playing fields'. In its base practice, Economics only shares benefits, or "why bother?", and has 'grown' best, when most needed.

REVENUES / RETURNS

As noted in any Economics course, or business book or manual, 'Revenue equals Price x Quantity (sold)'. This new paradigm of an Egg Model is not presented to contest economic theories or practiced business methods, merely to further assist the Science of Economics and to benefit world-wide possibilities of financial growth and learning, and to hopefully and humbly, gain in 'Revenues' for "the author himself".

Revenue or as loosely defined here as 'Returns'- from Sales, or returns on investments of Capital, Labor, Land, or Knowledge (me, the author), is 'The Shell' of the Economic Egg Model. It is the security, the beginning and end of business thoughts and practices, and sometimes 'the definer' of a Firm or 'Health' of an Economy.

Revenue is better explained by those 'in business' who have a 'track records' of year-over-year profits and, as our current President of these United States has done, conferring with successful 'Business Leaders', is essential to the on-going 'study' of Economics. Revenue, if solid and built upon 'sturdy foundations', is the cornerstone and 'key-stone' of Capitalism, De-Centralized Economies and dare, all "Developed Nations". Beyond all current information, history and thoughts, is beyond the focus and scope of this writing.

Revenue builds a 'housing' which holds 'in' all Economic Modes and Methods currently utilized. It guides and also determines a Firms future and the 'state' of an Economy, in the Aggregate. A steady Increasing Revenue 'Schedule', for a business as well as in Macro-Theory, positively grows 'Confidence' or 'General Positive Expectations', and allows for an overall 'good-sense / Positivity' Expectation for future Economics. Revenue Growth 'leaves room' for the other measures to grow also, 'Positive Supply Growth' furthering 'Labor Demand', 'Consumption' and 'Price Level' stabilization and 'slow-growth', "Expansion" on all levels.

TAXATION

'Taxes' or 'Taxation' is "The Air Bubble" present in every 'chicken's egg', at the 'fat bottom' of the egg. It is surmised, that it gives extra security and protective 'bounce', should 'the egg' fall too hard from the chicken.

Taxation, a very important 'Revenue Gather-er' of Governments and Social Bodies, in this 'Egg' shows the effects of 'Expanded Taxation', as in Monetary Theory, the more taxes "taken out", the less for Consumption or Savings. The opposite is true for 'less taxes', as the "air pocket" shrinks, so does 'Protection" and 'Overall Stability'. This can be shown in any society where less 'public goods and services' are present, 'slow emergency responses', 'less government oversight', 'non-descript government or leader', and so on and so on. It is also might be side-noted, that while "Ham and Eggs" go great together, 'overwrought pork-barreling and rotten eggs' do not.

WEALTH

'Wealth', like money, in economic terms, is hard-defined. It has been called, "the great divider", "nice if you can get it," and even 'Easy Street'. But, in Economics, it is still broad term meaning 'that which holds value to all'. Even water, in times of shortages or natural disasters, can be economically termed 'Wealth' if it is good, usable and collected. One's own water, for 'Consumption', to sustain life, would probably not be considered 'wealth' as selling it or trading-it away, all circumstances being held equal, would be *really* 'irrational' behavior and it is *Assumed* that one does not 'Economically engage' when one is dead, but then again, this is a modern and culturally detersive theory.

Our 'Economic Egg' puts Wealth as an egg's 'Blastodisc' or 'Germinal Disc', where the sperm fertilizes the ovum or egg. This "reproduction" of Wealth is still in an indeterminate and incubated state.

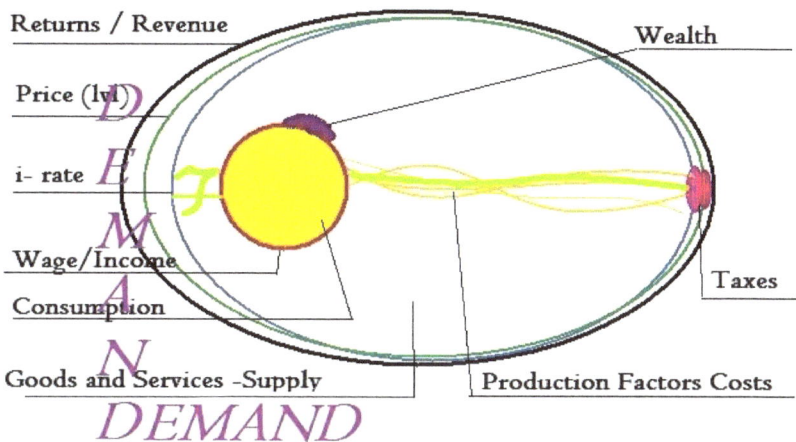

Full

model of the 'Economic Egg' –E.S.M. October 24, 2014

'SHOCKS' AND SHIFTS

As earlier discussed, movements from one Schedule effect another, 'Wealth' affecting Wage/Income, Supply, Consumption, Returns/Revenue, Price (Price Levels), even Interest (or interest-rates), and so forth. To illustrate, by 'Imagination', imagine a 'growth spurt' in Wages, say by about less than 40% of a 'minimum wage', this sudden 'shock' to the Wage Schedule or the 'Yolk Sack' will quickly and vigorously expand this measure, thereby also expanding Consumption, which in-turn, would expand Demand for Supply and therefore the Factors of Supply, Labor, (and perhaps Land, Knowledge and Capital Investment), and continue a "growth pattern" for the full Economy. Likewise if Demand were expanding from around our Economic Egg, exogenously, this would also 'leave room' for expansion and Growth, 'uplifting' all Schedules.

What we had, and continue to suffer from, the 2006-2007 global-fiscal contraction, from many international sources, Japan's Stagnation from its deflationary 'lost decades' period, The United States' "easy credit" policies, with less oversight and decreased-staffing of Agencies, European and Middle Eastern Disparities and continual African "malaises"", from both from within the Region and from World Entities as well as sure mismanagement, disparities of income gains, reporting, and International involvements as well as 'Over Enthusiasm' from not only all Latin Markets of "Latin Countries" but from all, in short, we are all 'to blame'.

This continued 'hit-or-miss', experimental 'punch-bowls', that World Financial Leaders have used to "dig-us-out" of the 2008 Global Economic and Fiscal Crisis and subsiding global panics, are by the inventors' own admissions, not meant to create our new systems of stable and sustainable economic foundations for a 'Global Economy'.

This 'Economic Egg' or 'Egg of Economics', 'Egg Model', what have you, is meant to help us all better understand and utilize an inclusive Economic system for "Nature and Mankind", "The Nature of Man", or "Mankind's place and footprint upon the World (and Star-Maps)". It is only a part of 'The Struggle' or 'Study' of an ongoing science-thought-proof, re-proof of "what is", "why", "what" and "what if", for us all, and what "We" can become!

It is this author's hope, and faith, that this Study of Trade, this Science of Economics will continue to thrill, perplex and excite those brave and intense "analytical minds" that dare to dream in 'the dismal', to continue-on with our thought-experiments and "Inquiries" into "the Natures Of…" for our heralded and much weighted Economic Systems. This, akin with every other discipline in Academics and human behavior, is open for debate.

Peace and prosperity to all. Please, invite me over for more than just omelets and egg creams, E.S.M.

BIBLIOGRAPHY

AUTHORS UTILIZED IN THIS WORK:

www.ingramcontent.com/pod-product-compliance
Lightning Source LLC
Chambersburg PA
CBHW041623180526
45159CB00002BC/995